The Key Facts™ on Malaysia

~Essential Information on Malaysia~

By Patrick W. Nee

The Internationalist®
www.internationalist.com

The Internationalist®

International Business, Investment, and Travel

Published by:

The Internationalist Publishing Company

96 Walter Street/ Suite 200

Boston, MA 02131, USA

Tel: 617-354-7722

www.internationalist.com

PN@internationalist.com

Copyright © 2014 by PWN

The Internationalist is a Registered Trademark. "Key Facts" and "The Internationalist Business Guides" are Trademarks of The Internationalist Publishing Company.

All Rights are reserved under International, Pan-American, and Pan-Asian Conventions. No part of this book may be reproduced in any form without the written permission of the publisher. All rights vigorously enforced

Table Of Contents

Chapter 1: Background
Chapter 2: Geography
Chapter 3: People and Society
Chapter 4: Government and Key Leaders
Chapter 5: Economy
Chapter 6: Energy
Chapter 7: Communications
Chapter 8: Transportation
Chapter 9: Military
Chapter 10: Transnational Issues
Map of Malaysia

Chapter 1: Background

During the late 18th and 19th centuries, Great Britain established colonies and protectorates in the area of current Malaysia; these were occupied by Japan from 1942 to 1945. In 1948, the British-ruled territories on the Malay Peninsula except Singapore formed the Federation of Malaya, which became independent in 1957. Malaysia was formed in 1963 when the former British colonies of Singapore, as well as Sabah and Sarawak on the northern coast of Borneo, joined the Federation. The first several years of the country's independence were marred by a Communist insurgency, Indonesian confrontation with Malaysia, Philippine claims to Sabah, and Singapore's withdrawal in 1965. During the 22-year term of Prime Minister MAHATHIR bin Mohamad (1981-2003), Malaysia was successful in diversifying its economy from dependence on exports of raw materials to the development of manufacturing, services, and tourism. Prime Minister Mohamed NAJIB bin Abdul Razak (in office since April 2009) has continued these pro-business policies and has introduced some civil reforms.

Chapter 2: Geography

Location:
    Southeastern Asia, peninsula bordering Thailand and northern one-third of the island of Borneo, bordering Indonesia, Brunei, and the South China Sea, south of Vietnam

Geographic coordinates:
    2 30 N, 112 30 E

Map references:
    Southeast Asia

Area:
    total: 329,847 sq km
    country comparison to the world: 67
    land: 328,657 sq km
    water: 1,190 sq km

Area - comparative:
    slightly larger than New Mexico

Land boundaries:
    total: 2,669 km
    border countries: Brunei 381 km, Indonesia 1,782 km, Thailand 506 km

Coastline:
    4,675 km (Peninsular Malaysia 2,068 km, East Malaysia 2,607 km)

Maritime claims:
    territorial sea: 12 nm
    exclusive economic zone: 200 nm
    continental shelf: 200 m depth or to the depth of exploitation; specified boundary in the South China Sea

Climate:
    tropical; annual southwest (April to October) and northeast (October to February) monsoons

Terrain:
    coastal plains rising to hills and mountains

Elevation extremes:
>lowest point: Indian Ocean 0 m
>
>highest point: Gunung Kinabalu 4,100 m

Natural resources:
>tin, petroleum, timber, copper, iron ore, natural gas, bauxite

Land use:
>arable land: 5.44%
>
>permanent crops: 17.49%
>
>other: 77.07% (2011)

Irrigated land:
>3,800 sq km (2009)

Total renewable water resources:
>580 cu km (2011)

Freshwater withdrawal (domestic/industrial/agricultural):
>total: 11.2 cu km/yr (35%/43%/22%)
>
>per capita: 414 cu m/yr (2005)

Natural hazards:
>flooding; landslides; forest fires

Environment - current issues:
>air pollution from industrial and vehicular emissions; water pollution from raw sewage; deforestation; smoke/haze from Indonesian forest fires

Environment - international agreements:
>party to: Biodiversity, Climate Change, Climate Change-Kyoto Protocol, Desertification, Endangered Species, Hazardous Wastes, Law of the Sea, Marine Life Conservation, Ozone Layer Protection, Ship Pollution, Tropical Timber 83, Tropical Timber 94, Wetlands
>
>signed, but not ratified: none of the selected agreements

Geography - note:
>strategic location along Strait of Malacca and southern South China Sea

Chapter 3: People and Society

Nationality:
>noun: Malaysian(s)
>adjective: Malaysian

Ethnic groups:
>Malay 50.4%, Chinese 23.7%, indigenous 11%, Indian 7.1%, others 7.8% (2004 est.)

Languages:
>Bahasa Malaysia (official), English, Chinese (Cantonese, Mandarin, Hokkien, Hakka, Hainan, Foochow), Tamil, Telugu, Malayalam, Panjabi, Thai
>note: in East Malaysia there are several indigenous languages; most widely spoken are Iban and Kadazan

Religions:
>Muslim (or Islam - official) 60.4%, Buddhist 19.2%, Christian 9.1%, Hindu 6.3%, Confucianism, Taoism, other traditional Chinese religions 2.6%, other or unknown 1.5%, none 0.8% (2000 census)

Population:
>29,628,392 (July 2013 est.)
>country comparison to the world: 43

Age structure:
>0-14 years: 29.1% (male 4,433,911/female 4,186,635)
>15-24 years: 17% (male 2,552,709/female 2,487,366)
>25-54 years: 41.3% (male 6,195,754/female 6,027,160)
>55-64 years: 7.4% (male 1,112,529/female 1,069,036)
>65 years and over: 5.3% (male 739,696/female 823,596) (2013 est.)

Median age:
>total: 27.4 years
>male: 27.2 years
>female: 27.6 years (2013 est.)

Population growth rate:
>1.51% (2013 est.)

country comparison to the world: 79

Birth rate:
20.41 births/1,000 population (2013 est.)

country comparison to the world: 83

Death rate:
4.97 deaths/1,000 population (2013 est.)

country comparison to the world: 184

Net migration rate:
-0.35 migrant(s)/1,000 population

country comparison to the world: 128

note: does not reflect net flow of an unknown number of illegal immigrants from other countries in the region (2013 est.)

Urbanization:
urban population: 72% of total population (2010)

rate of urbanization: 2.4% annual rate of change (2010-15 est.)

Major cities - population:
KUALA LUMPUR (capital) 1.493 million; Klang 1.071 million; Johor Bahru 958,000 (2009)

Sex ratio:
at birth: 1.07 male(s)/female

0-14 years: 1.06 male(s)/female

15-24 years: 1.03 male(s)/female

25-54 years: 1.03 male(s)/female

55-64 years: 1.05 male(s)/female

65 years and over: 0.89 male(s)/female

total population: 1.03 male(s)/female (2013 est.)

Maternal mortality rate:
29 deaths/100,000 live births (2010)

country comparison to the world: 125

Infant mortality rate:
total: 14.12 deaths/1,000 live births

country comparison to the world: 118

male: 16.32 deaths/1,000 live births

female: 11.77 deaths/1,000 live births (2013 est.)

Life expectancy at birth:

total population: 74.28 years

country comparison to the world: 112

male: 71.51 years

female: 77.24 years (2013 est.)

Total fertility rate:

2.61 children born/woman (2013 est.)

country comparison to the world: 78

Health expenditures:

4.4% of GDP (2010)

country comparison to the world: 156

Physicians density:

0.94 physicians/1,000 population (2008)

Hospital bed density:

1.8 beds/1,000 population (2010)

Drinking water source:

improved:

urban: 100% of population

rural: 99% of population

total: 100% of population

unimproved:

urban: 0% of population

rural: 1% of population

total: 0% of population (2010 est.)

Sanitation facility access:

improved:

urban: 96% of population

rural: 95% of population

total: 96% of population

unimproved:

urban: 4% of population

rural: 5% of population

total: 4% of population (2010 est.)

HIV/AIDS - adult prevalence rate:

0.5% (2009 est.)

country comparison to the world: 68

HIV/AIDS - people living with HIV/AIDS:

100,000 (2009 est.)

country comparison to the world: 41

HIV/AIDS - deaths:

5,800 (2009 est.)

country comparison to the world: 36

Major infectious diseases:

degree of risk: high

food or waterborne diseases: bacterial diarrhea

vectorborne diseases: dengue fever and malaria

note: highly pathogenic H5N1 avian influenza has been identified in this country; it poses a negligible risk with extremely rare cases possible among US citizens who have close contact with birds (2009)

Obesity - adult prevalence rate:

14% (2008)

country comparison to the world: 123

Children under the age of 5 years underweight:

12.9% (2006)

country comparison to the world: 58

Education expenditures:

5.1% of GDP (2010)

country comparison to the world: 70

Literacy:

definition: age 15 and over can read and write
total population: 88.7%
male: 92%
female: 85.4% (2000 census)

School life expectancy (primary to tertiary education):
total: 13 years
male: 12 years
female: 13 years (2008)

Unemployment, youth ages 15-24:
total: 11.3% (2010)
country comparison to the world: 103

Chapter 4: Government and Key Leaders

Country name:

    conventional long form: none

    conventional short form: Malaysia

    local long form: none

    local short form: Malaysia

    former: Federation of Malaya

Government type:

    constitutional monarchy

    note: nominally headed by paramount ruler (commonly referred to as the King) and a bicameral Parliament consisting of a nonelected upper house and an elected lower house; all Peninsular Malaysian states have hereditary rulers (commonly referred to as sultans) except Melaka (Malacca) and Pulau Pinang (Penang); those two states along with Sabah and Sarawak in East Malaysia have governors appointed by government; powers of state governments are limited by federal constitution; under terms of federation, Sabah and Sarawak retain certain constitutional prerogatives (e.g., right to maintain their own immigration controls)

Capital:

    name: Kuala Lumpur

    geographic coordinates: 3 10 N, 101 42 E

    time difference: UTC+8 (13 hours ahead of Washington, DC during Standard Time)

    note: Putrajaya is referred to as an administrative center not the capital; Parliament meets in Kuala Lumpur

Administrative divisions:

    13 states (negeri-negeri, singular - negeri); Johor, Kedah, Kelantan, Melaka, Negeri Sembilan, Pahang, Perak, Perlis, Pulau Pinang, Sabah, Sarawak, Selangor, Terengganu; and 1 federal territory (Wilayah Persekutuan) with 3 components, Kuala Lumpur, Labuan, and Putrajaya

Independence:

    31 August 1957 (from the UK)

National holiday:
>Independence Day 31 August (1957) (independence of Malaya); Malaysia Day 16 September (1963) (formation of Malaysia)

Constitution:
>31 August 1957; amended many times

Legal system:
>mixed legal system of English common law, Islamic law, and customary law; judicial review of legislative acts in the Supreme Court at request of supreme head of the federation

International law organization participation:
>has not submitted an ICJ jurisdiction declaration; non-party state to the ICCt

Suffrage:
>21 years of age; universal

Executive branch:
>chief of state: King - Tuanku ABDUL HALIM Mu'adzam Shah (selected on 13 December 2011; installed on 11 April 2012); the position of the king is primarily ceremonial
>
>head of government: Prime Minister Mohamed NAJIB bin Abdul Najib Razak (since 3 April 2009); Deputy Prime Minister MUHYIDDIN bin Mohamed Yassin (since 9 April 2009)
>
>cabinet: Cabinet appointed by the prime minister from among the members of Parliament with consent of the king
>
>elections: kings are elected by and from the hereditary rulers of nine of the states for five-year terms; selection is based on the principle of rotation among rulers of states; elections were last held on 14 October 2011 (next to be held in 2016); prime ministers are designated from among the members of the House of Representatives; following legislative elections, the leader who commands the support of the majority of members in the House becomes prime minister (since independence this has been the leader of the UMNO party)
>
>election results: Tuanku Abdul HALIM Mu'adzam Shah elected king by fellow hereditary rulers of nine states; Mohamed NAJIB bin Abdul Najib Razak was sworn in as

prime minister after former Prime Minister ABDULLAH Ahmad Badawi stepped down; ABDULLAH also stepped down as UMNO president; there was no party election for the post of president; the party passed the reins to NAJIB who was the deputy president

Legislative branch:

bicameral Parliament or Parlimen consists of Senate or Dewan Negara (70 seats; 44 members appointed by the king, 26 elected by 13 state legislatures to serve three-year terms with a two term limit) and House of Representatives or Dewan Rakyat (222 seats; members elected in 222 constituencies in a first-pass-the-post system to serve up to five-year terms)

elections: House of Representatives - last held on 8 March 2008 (next to be held on 5 May 2013)

election results: House of Representatives - percent of vote - BN coalition 50.3%, opposition parties 46.8%, others 2.9%; seats - BN coalition 140, opposition parties 82; (seats by party as of March 2013 - BN coalition 135, opposition parties 76, independents 11)

Judicial branch:

civil courts include Federal Court, Court of Appeal, High Court of Malaya on peninsula Malaysia, and High Court of Sabah and Sarawak in states of Borneo (judges are appointed by the king on the advice of the prime minister); sharia courts include Sharia Appeal Court, Sharia High Court, and Sharia Subordinate Courts at state-level and deal with religious and family matters such as custody, divorce, and inheritance only for Muslims; decisions of sharia courts cannot be appealed to civil courts

Political parties and leaders:

National Front (Barisan Nasional) or BN (ruling coalition) consists of the following parties: Gerakan Rakyat Malaysia Party or GERAKAN [KOH Tsu Koon]; Liberal Democratic Party (Parti Liberal Demokratik - Sabah) or LDP [LIEW Vui Keong]; Malaysian Chinese Association (Persatuan China Malaysia) or MCA [CHUA Soi Lek]; Malaysian Indian Congress (Kongres India Malaysia) or MIC [Govindasamy PALANIVEL]; Parti Bersatu Rakyat Sabah or PBRS [Joseph KURUP]; Parti Bersatu Sabah or PBS [Joseph PAIRIN Kitingan]; Parti Pesaka Bumiputera Bersatu or PBB [Abdul TAIB Mahmud]; Parti Rakyat Sarawak or PRS [James MASING]; Sarawak

United People's Party (Parti Bersatu Rakyat Sarawak) or SUPP [Peter CHIN Fah Kui];
United Malays National Organization or UMNO [NAJIB bin Abdul Razak]; United
Pasokmomogun Kadazandusun Murut Organization (Pertubuhan Pasko Momogun
Kadazan Dusun Bersatu) or UPKO [Bernard DOMPOK]; People's Progressive Party
(Parti Progresif Penduduk Malaysia) or PPP [M.Kayveas]

People's Alliance (Pakatan Rakyat) or PR (opposition coalition) consists of the following
parties: Democratic Action Party (Parti Tindakan Demokratik) or DAP [KARPAL Singh];
Islamic Party of Malaysia (Parti Islam se Malaysia) or PAS [Abdul HADI Awang];
People's Justice Party (Parti Keadilan Rakyat) or PKR [WAN AZIZAH Wan Ismail];
Sarawak National Party or SNAP [Edwin DUNDANG]

notable independent parties: Sabah Progressive Party (Parti Progresif Sabah) or SAPP
[YONG Teck Lee]; State Reform Pary (Parti Reformasi Negeri) or STAR [Jeffery
KITINGAN]

Political pressure groups and leaders:

Bar Council; BERSIH (electoral reform coalition); PEMBELA (Muslim NGO coalition);
PERKASA (defense of Malay rights)

other: religious groups; women's groups; youth groups

International organization participation:

ADB, APEC, ARF, ASEAN, BIS, C, CICA (observer), CP, D-8, EAS, FAO, G-15, G-77,
IAEA, IBRD, ICAO, ICC (national committees), ICRM, IDA, IDB, IFAD, IFC, IFRCS,
IHO, ILO, IMF, IMO, IMSO, Interpol, IOC, IPU, ISO, ITSO, ITU, ITUC (NGOs),
MIGA, MINURSO, MONUSCO, NAM, OIC, OPCW, PCA, PIF (partner), UN,
UNAMID, UNCTAD, UNESCO, UNIDO, UNIFIL, UNMIL, UNWTO, UPU, WCO,
WFTU (NGOs), WHO, WIPO, WMO, WTO

Diplomatic representation in the US:

chief of mission: Ambassador OTHMAN Bin Hashim
chancery: 3516 International Court NW, Washington, DC 20008
telephone: [1] (202) 572-9700
FAX: [1] (202) 572-9882
consulate(s) general: Los Angeles, New York

Diplomatic representation from the US:

chief of mission: Ambassador Paul W. JONES
embassy: 376 Jalan Tun Razak, 50400 Kuala Lumpur
mailing address: US Embassy Kuala Lumpur, APO AP 96535-8152
telephone: [60] (3) 2168-5000
FAX: [60] (3) 2148-5801

Key Leaders:

King	ABDUL HALIM Mu'adzam Shah
Prime Min.	NAJIB Razak
Dep. Prime Min.	MUHYIDDIN bin Mohamed Yassin
Min. of Agriculture & Agro-Based Industry	ISMAIL Sabri Yaakob
Min. of Communication & Multimedia	AHMAD SHABERY Cheek
Min. of Defense	HISHAMMUDDIN Tun Hussein
Min. of Domestic Trade, Cooperative, & Consumerism	HASAN Malek
Min. of Education & Higher Learning	MUHYIDDIN bin Mohamed Yassin
Min. of Education II	IDRIS Jusoh
Min. of Energy, Green Technology, & Water	Maximus Johnity ONGKILI
Min. of Federal Territories	Tengku ADNAN Tengku Mansor
Min. of Finance	NAJIB Razak
Min. of Finance II	AHMAD HUSNI Hanadzlah

Min. of Foreign Affairs	ANIFAH Aman
Min. of Health	S. SUBRAMANIAM
Min. of Home Affairs	Ahmad ZAHID Hamidi
Min. of Housing & Local Govt.	Abdul RAHMAN Dahlan
Min. of Human Resources	Richard RIOT Jaem
Min. of Intl. Trade & Industry	MUSTAPA Mohamed
Min. of Natural Resources & Environment	G. PALANIEVAL
Min. of Plantation Industries & Commodities	Douglas Unggah EMBAS
Min. of Rural Development & Territories	SHAFIE Apdal
Min. of Science, Technology, & Innovation	Ewon EBIN
Min. of Tourism & Culture	NAZRI Abdul Aziz
Min. of Transport (Acting)	HISHAMMUDDIN Tun Hussein
Min. of Women, Family, & Community Development	ROHANI Abdul Karim
Min. of Works	FADILLAH Yusof

Min. of Youth & Sports	KHAIRY Jamaluddin Abu Bakar
Min. in the Prime Min.'s Office	ABDUL WAHID Omar
Min. in the Prime Min.'s Office	Joseph ENTULU
Min. in the Prime Min.'s Office	Idris JALA
Min. in the Prime Min.'s Office	JAMIL KHIR bin Baharom, *Maj. Gen. (Ret.)*
Min. in the Prime Min.'s Office	Joseph KURUP
Min. in the Prime Min.'s Office	Paul LOW Seng Kuan
Min. in the Prime Min.'s Office	NANCY Shukri
Min. in the Prime Min.'s Office	SHAHIDAN Kassim
Governor, Bank Negara Malaysia	ZETI Akhtar Aziz
Ambassador to the US	OTHMAN Hashim
Permanent Representative to the UN, New York	Haniff HUSSEIN

Flag description:

14 equal horizontal stripes of red (top) alternating with white (bottom); there is a blue rectangle in the upper hoist-side corner bearing a yellow crescent and a yellow 14-pointed star; the flag is often referred to as Jalur Gemilang (Stripes of Glory); the 14 stripes stand for the equal status in the federation of the 13 member states and the federal

government; the 14 points on the star represent the unity between these entities; the crescent is a traditional symbol of Islam; blue symbolizes the unity of the Malay people and yellow is the royal color of Malay rulers

note: the design is based on the flag of the US

National symbol(s):

tiger

National anthem:

name: "Negaraku" (My Country)

lyrics/music: collective, led by Tunku ABDUL RAHMAN/Pierre Jean DE BERANGER

note: adopted 1957; the full version is only performed in the presence of the king; the tune, which was adopted from a popular French melody titled "La Rosalie," was originally the anthem of the state of Perak

Chapter 5: Economy

Economy - overview:

    Malaysia, a middle-income country, has transformed itself since the 1970s from a producer of raw materials into an emerging multi-sector economy. Under current Prime Minister NAJIB, Malaysia is attempting to achieve high-income status by 2020 and to move farther up the value-added production chain by attracting investments in Islamic finance, high technology industries, biotechnology, and services. NAJIB's Economic Transformation Program (ETP) is a series of projects and policy measures intended to accelerate the country's economic growth. The government has also taken steps to liberalize some services sub-sectors. The NAJIB administration also is continuing efforts to boost domestic demand and reduce the economy's dependence on exports. Nevertheless, exports - particularly of electronics, oil and gas, palm oil and rubber - remain a significant driver of the economy. As an oil and gas exporter, Malaysia has profited from higher world energy prices, although the rising cost of domestic gasoline and diesel fuel, combined with strained government finances, has forced Kuala Lumpur to begin to reduce government subsidies. The government is also trying to lessen its dependence on state oil producer Petronas. The oil and gas sector supplies about 35% of government revenue in 2011. Bank Negera Malaysia (central bank) maintains healthy foreign exchange reserves, and a well-developed regulatory regime has limited Malaysia's exposure to riskier financial instruments and the global financial crisis. Nevertheless, Malaysia could be vulnerable to a fall in commodity prices or a general slowdown in global economic activity because exports are a major component of GDP. In order to attract increased investment, NAJIB has raised possible revisions to the special economic and social preferences accorded to ethnic Malays under the New Economic Policy of 1970, but he has encountered significant opposition, especially from Malay nationalists and other vested interests.

GDP (purchasing power parity):

    $492.4 billion (2012 est.)

    <u>country comparison to the world</u>: 30

    $471.2 billion (2011 est.)

$448.4 billion (2010 est.)

note: data are in 2012 US dollars

GDP (official exchange rate):

$307.2 billion (2012 est.)

GDP - real growth rate:

4.5% (2012 est.)

country comparison to the world: 72

5.1% (2011 est.)

7.2% (2010 est.)

GDP - per capita (PPP):

$16,900 (2012 est.)

country comparison to the world: 79

$16,500 (2011 est.)

$15,900 (2010 est.)

note: data are in 2012 US dollars

GDP - composition by sector:

agriculture: 11.9%

industry: 41.2%

services: 46.8% (2012 est.)

Labor force:

12.92 million (2012 est.)

country comparison to the world: 42

Labor force - by occupation:

agriculture: 11.1%

industry: 36%

services: 53.5% (2012 est.)

Unemployment rate:

3.2% (2012 est.)

country comparison to the world: 26

3.1% (2011 est.)

Population below poverty line:

3.8% (2009 est.)

Household income or consumption by percentage share:

lowest 10%: 1.8%

highest 10%: 34.7% (2009 est.)

Distribution of family income - Gini index:

46.2 (2009)

country comparison to the world: 33

49.2 (1997)

Investment (gross fixed):

25.2% of GDP (2012 est.)

country comparison to the world: 50

Budget:

revenues: $59.22 billion

expenditures: $75.31 billion (2012 est.)

Taxes and other revenues:

19.3% of GDP (2012 est.)

country comparison to the world: 168

Budget surplus (+) or deficit (-):

-5.2% of GDP (2012 est.)

country comparison to the world: 161

Public debt:

53.5% of GDP (2012 est.)

country comparison to the world: 54

51.8% of GDP (2011 est.)

note: this figure is based on the amount of federal government debt, RM501.6 billion ($167.2 billion) in 2012; this includes Malaysian Treasury bills and other government securities, as well as loans raised externally and bonds and notes issued overseas; this figure excludes debt issued by non-financial public enterprises and guaranteed by the federal government, which was an additional $47.7 billion in 2012

Inflation rate (consumer prices):

1.9% (2012 est.)

country comparison to the world: 30

3.2% (2011 est.)

note: approximately 30% of goods are price-controlled

Central bank discount rate:

3% (31 December 2011)

country comparison to the world: 107

2.83% (31 December 2010)

Commercial bank prime lending rate:

4.9% (31 December 2012 est.)

country comparison to the world: 160

4.83% (31 December 2011 est.)

Stock of narrow money:

$96.68 billion (31 December 2012 est.)

country comparison to the world: 36

$81.28 billion (31 December 2011 est.)

Stock of broad money:

$458.5 billion (31 December 2012 est.)

country comparison to the world: 23

$382.2 billion (31 December 2011 est.)

Stock of domestic credit:

$403.7 billion (31 December 2012 est.)

country comparison to the world: 29

$354.6 billion (31 December 2011 est.)

Market value of publicly traded shares:

$414 billion (31 December 2011)

country comparison to the world: 23

$410.5 billion (31 December 2010)

$256 billion (31 December 2009)

Agriculture - products:

Peninsular Malaysia - palm oil, rubber, cocoa, rice; Sabah - palm oil, subsistence crops; rubber, timber; Sarawak - palm oil, rubber, timber; pepper

Industries:
>Peninsular Malaysia - rubber and oil palm processing and manufacturing, petroleum and natural gas, light manufacturing, pharmaceuticals, medical technology, electronics and semi-conductors, timber processing; Sabah - logging, petroleum and natural gas production; Sarawak - agriculture processing, petroleum and natural gas production, logging

Industrial production growth rate:
>1.4% (2011 est.)
>
>country comparison to the world: 129

Current account balance:
>$22.8 billion (2012 est.)
>
>country comparison to the world: 16
>
>$32.03 billion (2011 est.)

Exports:
>$247 billion (2012 est.)
>
>country comparison to the world: 24
>
>$227.5 billion (2011 est.)

Exports - commodities:
>semiconductors and electronic equipment, palm oil, petroleum and liquefied natural gas, wood and wood products, palm oil, rubber, textiles, chemicals, solar panels

Exports - partners:
>China 13.1%, Singapore 12.7%, Japan 11.5%, US 8.3%, Thailand 5.1%, Hong Kong 4.5%, India 4.1% (2011)

Imports:
>$202.4 billion (2012 est.)
>
>country comparison to the world: 27
>
>$178.6 billion (2011 est.)

Imports - commodities:
>electronics, machinery, petroleum products, plastics, vehicles, iron and steel products, chemicals

Imports - partners:

China 13.2%, Singapore 12.8%, Japan 11.4%, US 9.7%, Indonesia 6.1%, Thailand 6%, South Korea 4% (2011)

Reserves of foreign exchange and gold:
$140.4 billion (31 December 2012 est.)
country comparison to the world: 20
$133.6 billion (31 December 2011 est.)

Debt - external:
$95.55 billion (31 December 2012 est.)
country comparison to the world: 46
$89.71 billion (31 December 2011 est.)

Stock of direct foreign investment - at home:
$123 billion (31 December 2012 est.)
country comparison to the world: 33
$112.1 billion (31 December 2011 est.)

Stock of direct foreign investment - abroad:
$123.3 billion (31 December 2012 est.)
country comparison to the world: 27
$110.3 billion (31 December 2011 est.)

Exchange rates:

ringgits (MYR) per US dollar -
3.07 (2012 est.)
3.06 (2011 est.)
3.22 (2010 est.)
3.52 (2009)
3.33 (2008)

Fiscal year:
calendar year

Chapter 6: Energy

Electricity - production:
> 118 billion kWh (2012 est.)
> country comparison to the world: 31

Electricity - consumption:
> 112 billion kWh (2012 est.)
> country comparison to the world: 29

Electricity - exports:
> 88 million kWh (2010 est.)
> country comparison to the world: 73

Electricity - imports:
> 33 million kWh (2010 est.)
> country comparison to the world: 103

Electricity - installed generating capacity:
> 25.24 million kW (2009 est.)
> country comparison to the world: 32

Electricity - from fossil fuels:
> 91.7% of total installed capacity (2009 est.)
> country comparison to the world: 73

Electricity - from nuclear fuels:
> 0% of total installed capacity (2009 est.)
> country comparison to the world: 145

Electricity - from hydroelectric plants:
> 8.3% of total installed capacity (2009 est.)
> country comparison to the world: 118

Electricity - from other renewable sources:
> 0% of total installed capacity (2009 est.)
> country comparison to the world: 163

Crude oil - production:
> 603,400 bbl/day (2011 est.)

country comparison to the world: 29

Crude oil - exports:

269,000 bbl/day (2012 est.)

country comparison to the world: 27

Crude oil - imports:

199,100 bbl/day (2009 est.)

country comparison to the world: 34

Crude oil - proved reserves:

2.9 billion bbl (1 January 2013 es)

country comparison to the world: 30

Refined petroleum products - production:

649,700 bbl/day (2008 est.)

country comparison to the world: 28

Refined petroleum products - consumption:

542,900 bbl/day (2011 est.)

country comparison to the world: 34

Refined petroleum products - exports:

213,800 bbl/day (2008 est.)

country comparison to the world: 30

Refined petroleum products - imports:

178,200 bbl/day (2008 est.)

country comparison to the world: 29

Natural gas - production:

66.5 billion cu m (2010 est.)

country comparison to the world: 14

Natural gas - consumption:

35.7 billion cu m (2010 est.)

country comparison to the world: 27

Natural gas - exports:

31.99 billion cu m (2010 est.)

country comparison to the world: 13

Natural gas - imports:

2.94 billion cu m (2010 est.)

country comparison to the world: 44

Natural gas - proved reserves:

2.35 trillion cu m (1 January 2012 es)

country comparison to the world: 16

Carbon dioxide emissions from consumption of energy:

181.9 million Mt (2010 est.)

country comparison to the world: 30

Chapter 7: Communications

Telephones - main lines in use:
    4.243 million (2011)
    country comparison to the world: 40

Telephones - mobile cellular:
    36.661 million (2012)
    country comparison to the world: 30

Telephone system:
    general assessment: modern system featuring good intercity service on Peninsular Malaysia provided mainly by microwave radio relay and an adequate intercity microwave radio relay network between Sabah and Sarawak via Brunei; international service excellent
    domestic: domestic satellite system with 2 earth stations; combined fixed-line and mobile-cellular teledensity roughly 140 per 100 persons
    international: country code - 60; landing point for several major international submarine cable networks that provide connectivity to Asia, Middle East, and Europe; satellite earth stations - 2 Intelsat (1 Indian Ocean, 1 Pacific Ocean) (2011)

Broadcast media:
    state-owned TV broadcaster operates 2 TV networks with relays throughout the country, and the leading private commercial media group operates 4 TV stations with numerous relays throughout the country; satellite TV subscription service is available; state-owned radio broadcaster operates multiple national networks as well as regional and local stations; many private commercial radio broadcasters and some subscription satellite radio services are available; about 55 radio stations overall (2012)

Internet country code:
    .my

Internet hosts:
    422,470 (2012)
    country comparison to the world: 53

Internet users:

15.355 million (2009)

country comparison to the world: 26

Chapter 8: Transportation

Airports:
>117 (2012)
>country comparison to the world: 49

Airports - with paved runways:
>total: 39
>over 3,047 m: 8
>2,438 to 3,047 m: 9
>1,524 to 2,437 m: 6
>914 to 1,523 m: 8
>under 914 m: 8 (2012)

Airports - with unpaved runways:
>total: 78
>914 to 1,523 m: 7
>under 914 m: 71 (2012)

Heliports:
>3 (2012)

Pipelines:
>condensate 3 km; gas 1,757 km; liquid petroleum gas 155 km; oil 30 km; refined products 114 km (2010)

Railways:
>total: 1,849 km
>country comparison to the world: 75
>standard gauge: 57 km 1.435-m gauge (57 km electrified)
>narrow gauge: 1,792 km 1.000-m gauge (150 km electrified) (2008)

Roadways:
>total: 98,721 km
>country comparison to the world: 42
>paved: 80,280 km (includes 1,821 km of expressways)
>unpaved: 18,441 km (2004)

Waterways:

7,200 km (Peninsular Malaysia 3,200 km; Sabah 1,500 km; Sarawak 2,500 km) (2011)
country comparison to the world: 20

Merchant marine:

total: 315

country comparison to the world: 31

by type: bulk carrier 11, cargo 83, carrier 2, chemical tanker 47, container 41, liquefied gas 34, passenger/cargo 4, petroleum tanker 86, roll on/roll off 2, vehicle carrier 5

foreign-owned: 26 (Denmark 1, Hong Kong 8, Japan 2, Russia 2, Singapore 13)

registered in other countries: 82 (Bahamas 13, India 1, Indonesia 1, Isle of Man 6, Malta 1, Marshall Islands 11, Panama 12, Papua New Guinea 1, Philippines 1, Saint Kitts and Nevis 1, Singapore 27, Thailand 3, US 2, unknown 2) (2010)

Ports and terminals:

Bintulu, Johor Bahru, George Town (Penang), Port Kelang (Port Klang), Tanjung Pelepas

Transportation - note:

the International Maritime Bureau reports that the territorial and offshore waters in the Strait of Malacca and South China Sea remain high risk for piracy and armed robbery against ships; in the past, commercial vessels have been attacked and hijacked both at anchor and while underway; hijacked vessels are often disguised and cargo diverted to ports in East Asia; crews have been murdered or cast adrift; increased naval patrols since 2005 in the Strait of Malacca resulted in no reported incidents in 2010

Chapter 9: Military

Military branches:

Malaysian Armed Forces (Angkatan Tentera Malaysia, ATM): Malaysian Army (Tentera Darat Malaysia), Royal Malaysian Navy (Tentera Laut Diraja Malaysia, TLDM), Royal Malaysian Air Force (Tentera Udara Diraja Malaysia, TUDM) (2010)

Military service age and obligation:

17 years 6 months of age for voluntary military service (younger with parental consent and proof of age); mandatory retirement age 60; women serve in the Malaysian Armed Forces; no conscription (2013)

Manpower available for military service:

males age 16-49: 7,501,518

females age 16-49: 7,315,999 (2010 est.)

Manpower fit for military service:

males age 16-49: 6,247,306

females age 16-49: 6,175,274 (2010 est.)

Manpower reaching militarily significant age annually:

male: 265,008

female: 254,812 (2010 est.)

Military expenditures:

2.03% of GDP (2005 est.)

country comparison to the world: 65

Chapter 10: Transnational Issues

Disputes - international:
> while the 2002 "Declaration on the Conduct of Parties in the South China Sea" has eased tensions over the Spratly Islands, it is not the legally binding "code of conduct" sought by some parties; Malaysia was not party to the March 2005 joint accord among the national oil companies of China, the Philippines, and Vietnam on conducting marine seismic activities in the Spratly Islands; disputes continue over deliveries of fresh water to Singapore, Singapore's land reclamation, bridge construction, and maritime boundaries in the Johor and Singapore Straits; in 2008, ICJ awarded sovereignty of Pedra Branca (Pulau Batu Puteh/Horsburgh Island) to Singapore, and Middle Rocks to Malaysia, but did not rule on maritime regimes, boundaries, or disposition of South Ledge; land and maritime negotiations with Indonesia are ongoing, and disputed areas include the controversial Tanjung Datu and Camar Wulan border area in Borneo and the maritime boundary in the Ambalat oil block in the Celebes Sea; separatist violence in Thailand's predominantly Muslim southern provinces prompts measures to close and monitor border with Malaysia to stem terrorist activities; Philippines retains a dormant claim to Malaysia's Sabah State in northern Borneo; Per Letters of Exchange signed in 2009, Malaysia in 2010 ceded two hydrocarbon concession blocks to Brunei in exchange for Brunei's sultan dropping claims to the Limbang corridor, which divides Brunei; piracy remains a problem in the Malacca Strait

Refugees and internally displaced persons:
> refugees (country of origin): 81,146 (Burma) (2011)

Trafficking in persons:
> <u>current situation</u>: Malaysia is a destination and, to a lesser extent, a source and transit country for women and children trafficked for the purpose of commercial sexual exploitation, and men, women, and children for forced labor; Malaysia is mainly a destination country for men, women, and children who migrate willingly from countries including Indonesia, Nepal, India, Thailand, China, the Philippines, Burma, Cambodia, Bangladesh, Pakistan, and Vietnam to work, some of whom are subjected to conditions of involuntary servitude by Malaysian employers in the domestic, agricultural, construction,

plantation, and industrial sectors; a small number of Malaysian citizens were reportedly trafficked internally and abroad to Singapore, China, and Japan for commercial sexual exploitation

<u>tier rating</u>: Tier 2 Watch List - the Government of Malaysia does not fully comply with the minimum standards for the elimination of trafficking; however, it is making significant efforts to do so; while the government increased the number of convictions obtained under the Anti-Trafficking in Persons and Anti-Smuggling of Migrants Act during the year and continued public awareness efforts on trafficking, it did not effectively investigate and prosecute labor trafficking cases, and failed to address problems of government complicity in trafficking and lack of effective victim care and counseling by authorities (2009)

Illicit drugs:

drug trafficking prosecuted vigorously and carries severe penalties; heroin still primary drug of abuse, but synthetic drug demand remains strong; continued ecstasy and methamphetamine producer for domestic users and, to a lesser extent, the regional drug market

Map of Malaysia

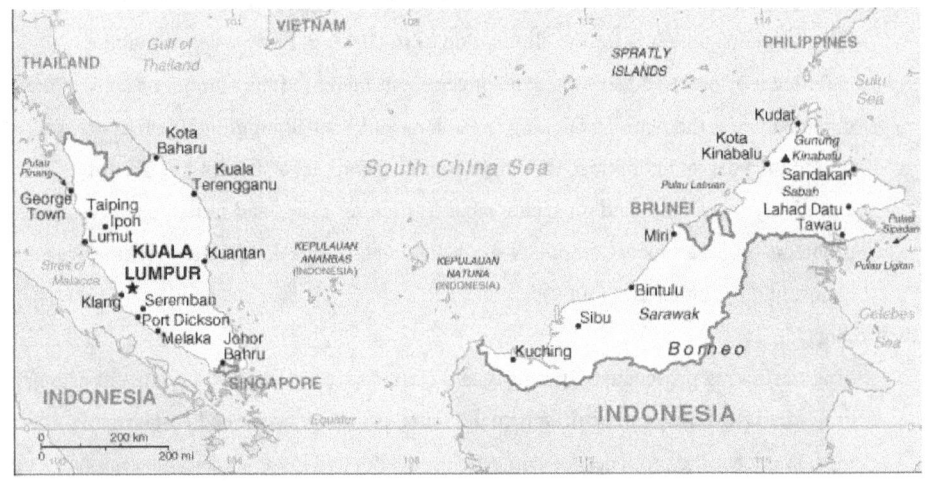

Other Key Facts™ Titles

Key Facts on Syria

Key Facts on China

Key Facts on Qatar

Key Facts on India

Key Facts on Germany

Key Facts on Argentina

Key Facts on Russia

Key Facts on North Korea

Key Facts on Brazil

Key Facts on Italy

Key Facts on the United Arab Emirates

Key Facts on the European Union

Key Facts on Pakistan

Key Facts on Saudi Arabia

Key Facts on Cyprus

Key Facts on Iran

Key Facts on Afghanistan

Key Facts on Iraq

Key Facts on Indonesia

Key Facts on South Korea

Key Facts on France

Key Facts on the United Kingdom

Key Facts on Egypt

Key Facts on Israel

Key Facts on Mexico

Key Facts on the United States of America

Key Facts on Turkey

Key Facts on South Africa

Key Facts on Greece

Key Facts on Japan

All Key Facts™ Titles are Available at www.Amazon.com

THE INTERNATIONALIST®
2013
WWW.INTERNATIONALIST.COM

www.ingramcontent.com/pod-product-compliance
Lightning Source LLC
Chambersburg PA
CBHW070722180526
45167CB00004B/1583